Strolls & Walks from Picnic Places

A short stroll and a 4 or 5 mile walk
from twenty one picnic places in
Warwickshire, Worcestershire,
Staffordshire & Shropshire

by John Roberts
with cartoons & sketches by Liz Johnson

****
WALKWAYS
J S Roberts
8 Hillside Close, Bartley Green
Birmingham B32 4LT
****

Strolls & Walks
from
PICNIC PLACES

by John Roberts
with illustrations by Liz Johnson

ISBN 0 947708 27 8

First Published 1992

Printed on recycled paper.

WALKWAYS

DaywalkS Footpath Networks

Sets of short footpath routes which are linked to make networks of connected circular walks. The last three are in book form, the rest are A2 sheets folded down to A5. All come in plastic covers.

Arden
Cannock Chase
Chaddesley Woods
Clent & Lickey Hills
Elan Valley
Wyre Forest
Vale of Llangollen
Bridgnorth - Kinver - Stourport

Long Distance Routes

Step by step guides in both directions with sketch maps. They often connect with each other and other Long Distance Footpaths. All are A2 sheets folded to A5, but Heart of England Way is a book.

Llangollen to Bala
Bala to Snowdon
Birmingham to Ludlow
Ludlow to Rhayader
Rhayader to Aberystwyth
Birmingham to Church Stretton
Heart of England Way

8 Hillside Close, Bartley Green, Birmingham B32 4LT
(Send sae for current list & prices.)

To enjoy the best of the countryside

Join The Ramblers.

Explore the many hundreds of thousands of miles of Britain's beautiful footpaths and receive our exclusive Yearbook full of information on walking and places to stay.

Plus regular colour magazines and newsletters — free of charge.

You will also be entitled to valuable discounts at outdoor equipment shops.

And at the same time you wi be helping us to protect th countryside and to look afte Britain's footpath

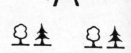

The Pedestrians Association
"WalkWays" Campaign

This venerable organisation was founded in 1929 to promote safety for walkers in towns and cities. They argue for such things as zebra crossings, wide pavements, traffic bollards and speed bumps.

In 1992 they launched a campaign to help people and groups run their own campaigns on neighbourhood issues, with an advice pack, telephone helpline and consultancy backup. And they had the brilliant idea of calling it "WalkWays".

The Pedestrians Association had never heard of my WALKWAYS Publishing and I had only the dimmest idea about them, but we both thought is was funny and agreed to support one another. You should support them too. Motorists have influential organisations, think of the numbers of pedestrians.

You can reach the Pedestrians Association at 1 Wandsworth Road, London SW8 2XX, 071 735 3270.

Contents

Picnic Places

You would think that there would be lots of places
where you could picnic all over the Midlands. But
heavily farmed countryside is not like the
mountains and moors, you can't just plonk yourself
anywhere. Woods, ponds, streams and river banks
may have footpaths through them, but the land is
private. Most of the suitable places turned out to
be Country Parks and the like set up by Councils or
people such as Severn Trent Water. There are some
Commons and the Woodland Trust have allowed me to
use one of their woods. I have tried to find less
well known sites, so have not used the very popular
ones, such as Kinver Edge or the Clent Hills. Do
not expect tables and chairs, some places have them
but you may have to sit on the rug.

From most of the picnic places I have described a
walk of between 4 and 6 miles, and because some
people are young with short legs, or old with tired
ones, there is also a stroll.

The Country Code

* Enjoy the countryside and respect its life and work
* Guard against all risk of fire
* Fasten all gates
* Keep your dogs under close control
* Keep to public paths across farmland
* Use gates and stiles to cross fences, hedges and
                                        walls
* Leave livestock, crops and machinery alone
* Take your litter home
* Help to keep water clean
* Protect wildlife, plants and trees
* Take special care on country roads
* Make no uneccessary noise

Picnic Places

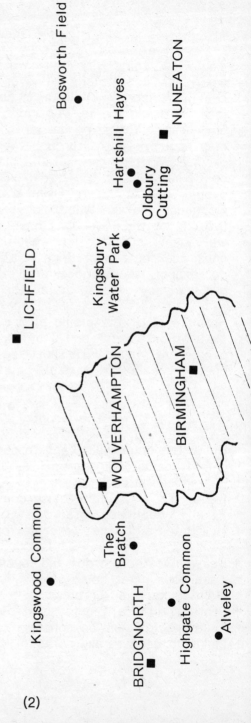

STAFFORD

Seven Springs

Castle Ring

LICHFIELD

Bosworth Field

Hartshill Hayes

NUNEATON

Oldbury Cutting

Kingsbury Water Park

WOLVERHAMPTON

BIRMINGHAM

Kingswood Common

The Bratch

BRIDGNORTH

Highgate Common

Alveley

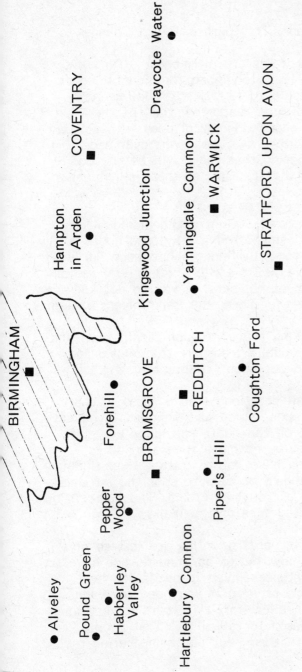

BIRMINGHAM

Forehill

Pepper
Wood

Alveley

Pound Green

Habberley
Valley

Hartlebury Common

BROMSGROVE

Piper's Hill

REDDITCH

Coughton Ford

Hampton
in Arden

Kingswood Junction

Yarningdale Common

WARWICK

COVENTRY

Draycote Water

STRATFORD UPON AVON

Milcote

*
*
*
*
*

Clothing, Maps, Transport & Route Changes

These strolls and walks are all modest affairs and you do not need to go equipped for mountaineering. Trainers are suitable footwear, with wellies for wet weather. The most important part of the footwear is socks; get thick wool ones with a loop pile if possible. Otherwise, wear whatever seems sensible, remembering that there will be the odd boggy patch and that in summer there might be brambles and nettles.

I have described the location of the picnic places which are usually signposted locally, and added a map reference. You will find the Ordnance Survey Landranger maps (1.25ins/1mile - 2cms/1km) useful and I give the sheet numbers. If you do not know how to use map references, the Landrangers explain.

There is car parking space at each picnic spot, and I have noted any public transport that exists and how you can find out about timetables.

The routes are all described step by step in short numbered paragraphs, which are designed to be easy to find and read on the hoof. The maps are quite rough and offered as no more than a guide to placing where you have got to, rather than finding your way. You should be able to spot the streams, lanes, ponds etc as you meet them. The numbers on the maps are paragraphs of the Walk.

Distances given in yards or miles are just to give you an IDEA of how far to go. You do not have try and measure. Distances given in paces can be counted out (more or less) if you need to. Paces vary but you can allow for it if yours is very long or short. The reason for all this is that people carry a pace with them, but not a measuring tape.

These walks are on public rights of way or well established paths and tracks. They were all clear of obstructions when we went to press, but the countryside changes all the time. You could meet new tracks, stiles, gates and barns; hedges vanish, paths are diverted and trees fall down. To keep directions up to date I issue amendment slips.

IF you write to tell me of any changes or problems that you meet, stating route and paragraph number, I will refund your postage.

IF you send me a stamped addressed envelope with a note of what publication(s) you have, I will send you up to date amendment slips.

List of Picnic Places

Main Map Symbols

Picnic place	●	Walk/Stroll	◄ᵂ ▻ˢ
Path	··········	Track	- - ᵜ -᷍ ᷍
Road/lane	‿‿‿	Railway	+-+-+ - ⊢ ⊣ - ⊢-
			disused
Canal	⊥ ⊥ ⊥	Stream	⌇⌇⌇
River/lake	⬳	Woodland	▰▰▰

Alveley

WHERE
Map reference SO 754839, Landranger 138 Kidder-
-minster & Wyre Forest. A Country Park by the River
Severn near ALVELEY on the A442.

Buses run through Alveley and Highley - details
0345 256785. Severn Valley Railway steam trains run
from Bridgnorth, Bewdley and Kidderminster to
Highley Station .75 miles downstream of the Park
(enquires - 0299 403816). From the station follow
the river bank upstream and cross the first bridge.

PARK & PICNIC
Ample parking, picnic anywhere, but there are
tables within sight of the Visitor Centre. Railway
nutters could try the tables at the far end of the
stroll, near enough to the trains to get coal dust
in your butties. WC's

SEVERN VALLEY COUNTRY PARK
Opened in June 1992 by Bridgnorth District Council,
the Visitor Centre was still in the building when I
wrote this. The 160 acre park is on both sides of
the valley, on the east bank a majestic slope
diving 300 feet from a ridge to the river.

The grass on the lower half is thick and green, but
above the Centre it struggles through thin black
grit. The whole site is reclaimed from the waste
tips of Alveley and Highley Collieries which
closed in 1969. Some of the buildings and a small
industrial estate lie on the north side to remind
you that the Industrial Revolution started in this

gorgous landscape. But the estate is out of sight and the sparse growth on the upper levels will produce a richness of wildflowers through the strange mix of acid and alkaline soils. Even now there is a healthy crowd of butterflies, Small Tortoiseshell, Peacock, Comma, Brimstone, Green Veined White, Small Heath, Common Blue, Small Copper, with dragon and damsel flies.

The views of the valley and the broad river are superb, but the vistas from the higher points and especially the Walk are even better. Beyond the green valley are ranges of wooded hills, and on the far skyline, Titterstone and Brown Clee to the west, the Wrekin further north and to the south west, the Abberley Hills.

The first Severn Valley Railway lasted from 1858 to 1963 and ran between Shrewsbury and Hartlebury, just south of Kidderminster. The valley coal output which was an important part of the traffic ceased in 1960, and Dr Beeching did not blink. (Surely the Doctor is now a folk figure like Guy Fawkes, Boney and the Green Man). The SVR Society was founded in 1965 and had reopened the line between Bewdley and Brignorth by 1974, and the link to Kidderminster in 1984. Highley station is just downstream from the Park. Cross the bridge and follow the river bank.

THE STROLL
You can wander up and down the little paths round the park and you don't need me for that. But it may not be obvious that the Park covers both banks of the river. Here is a wander of 1.25 miles with an alternative railwayside picnic site.

(1) From Visitor Centre take path down (& bearing R) to river. Cross bridge.

(2) Bear R & take track on L side of "Motorcycles" sign to picnic site.

(3) Leave site via steps down to river. Follow bank back to bridge and return to Centre. ●

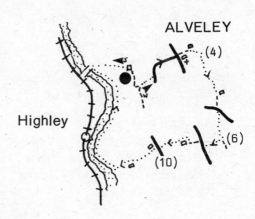

ALVELEY

Highley

(4)

(6)

(10)

THE WALK

These 4 miles are almost the best in the book for views and scenery. The vista of the silver Severn, the deep green valley at your feet and the hills to the horizon is magical. And you can see a tiny chapel built in 1862, which must have been quite isolated, a string of meadows, a sandstone farm perched on the rim of the valley and surrounded by hawthorne and may, and a romantic ruin by an old quarry pit. The ruin is one of my favourite places, tumbled but serene - watching the river.

(1) Leave Visitor Centre by main exit drive. Pass between ponds R & L to R bend, then take small gate ahead.

(2) Go up via next gate & keep same line to top gate & lane. Go L, round R bend, to T junction.

(3) Take path L of chapel, at house gate go R of fence & follow to stile & field. ◀

(4) Go ahead down field edge to corner stile (DON'T TAKE IT). Go R with hedge on your L, via stiles to open field.

(5) Cross midfield bearing L towards end of red brick barn, & take stile. Take next stile then track to lane.

(6) Take gate/stile opposite & go with hedge on your L 3 fields, to stile at end of green lane. (DON'T TAKE IT) ▶

(7) Go R up field edge to stile & lane. Go R a few paces & cross stile by farm gate. Follow track to next gate.

(8) Take stiles (1) & (2), then go R with shed on your L & take stile (3). Go L along fence, pass house & on appx 200 yds to take stile L. ◀

(9) Go down field edge & take stile R. Continue down hedge to corner & cross via telephone poles to gate & lane.

(10) Go R a few paces & take gate opposite. Go with hedge on your R via 2 gates, pass ruin & down to river.

(11) Take stile R, follow bank to bridge & return to Visitor Centre. ●

Bosworth Field

WHERE
Map reference SP 411994, Landranger 140 Leicester &
Coventry. The site of the Battle of Bosworth, 2
miles south of Market Bosworth. (From A5 south of
ATHERSTONE take Fenny Drayton road for 5.5 miles to
canal and car park.) Bus details 0455 290429.

PARK & PICNIC
The Battlefield is managed by Leicestershire County
Council. There are three car parks and these walks
start from the canalside park at Sutton Cheney
Wharf. You can picnic at the wharf or walk through
Ambion Wood and picnic near the Visitor Centre,
where there are WC's.

THE PLACE
Ambion Hill at about 350 feet dominates a flat
green plain. It is the only place and the
essential place for an army to defend. In August
1485 a force lead by Henry Tudor challenged King
Richard III's position. Illustrated boards and
richly coloured standards drooping from flagpoles
in the fields show the positions of the troops. You
can find out all about it at the Visitor Centre.
(Henry won by quite lot nil.)

Bosworth was one of the definitive events in
English history and marked not only the end of the
civil Wars of the Roses but of the whole mediaeval
period. English government would in future be
strong and central and take on some of its modern
form. In this same few years at the end of the
1400's William Caxton started his printing press

and Columbus sailed to the New World. This period is the hinge between two ages.

Sutton Cheney Wharf is on the 22 mile Ashby Canal from Snarestone through Market Bosworth and Hinckley to join the Coventry Canal. First planned as a link from Coventry to the River Trent, it remained just a southern outlet for local limestone and coal. The Ashby curls placidly through the site of the great battle, on which it had little influence, since it was built in 1802.

The Market Bosworth Light Railway is steam hauled and standard gauge running the 5 miles from Snackerstone via Market Bosworth to Shenton beside the Battlefield. It is a section of the old Midland Railway line from Nuneaton towards Burton on Trent which was abandoned in the 1960's. The Midland owned the canal and they run beside each other.

TWO WALKS
You can stroll round the Battlefield Trail and you don't need me for that, so I offer Walk (A) of about 5 miles, and a curtailed version, Walk (B) of 3.5 miles. Both start at Sutton Cheney Wharf and pass through the Battlefield.

WALKS (A) & (B)

*

(1) From canalside picnic site take marked path (blue & yellow square) along canal & thro wood to Visitor Centre.

(2) Leave on Battlefield Trail via far upper corner of car park & follow it to railway.

(3) Cross line & exit to lane. Go R past King Richard's Field & take 1st lane L to bridge.

(4) Go under it & take steps L to towpath. Facing canal, go R appx .5 mile & under 1st bridge

WALK(B)

(4i) Continue on canal appx 1.25 miles to wharf & start.

WALK (A) continues:

(5) From bridge, exit R to lane. Go ahead, round L bend & take 1st track R to farm. ◢

(6) Just before farm, take stile R & fenced path to stile & field. Go ahead across brook to gate R. DON'T TAKE IT.

(7) Go L parallel with brook & take stile. Sight R end of big trees & head for stile on its R (yellow mark).

(8) Cross stile & go with hedge on your L to take corner stile. Cross yard & take stile, then paddock ditto, to big field.

(9) Go parallel with drive R & take stile to road.

(10) Go L to x roads, then R to canal bridge & join towpath.

(11) Go L appx 1.5 miles to Bridge 54 & car park etc. ●

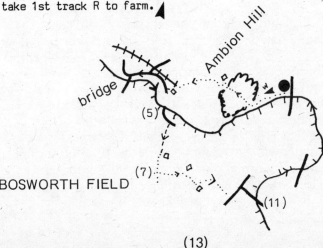

Ambion Hill

bridge

(5)

(7)

(11)

BOSWORTH FIELD

(13)

The Bratch

WHERE
Map reference SO 868937, Landranger 139 Birmingham.
Locks on the Staffordshire & Worcestershire Canal
north east of WOMBOURNE, near Wolverhampton. Buses
run - details 0785 223344.

PARK & PICNIC
There is a clearly marked car park and a canal side
site with seats, courtesy of Severn Trent Water.

THE LOCKS, THE PUMPHOUSE & THE RAILWAY
Bratch Locks are quaint and delightful with an
octagonal toll office. They raise the canal about
30 feet and look terribly complicated, but are
simply three separate locks. The worst problem is
that boats have to pass all three at once, which
can cause a queue in the height of the season. The
solution is not to build a by pass, but to stop
caring and have another lie down on the cabin top
until it is your turn. The Staffs & Worcs Canal was
opened in 1772 and runs 46 miles from the Trent &
Mersey Canal near Stafford to the River Severn.

By the picnic site is a gingerbread castle, shiny
bright in red Ruabon brick with tiny corner
turrets, pointed arched windows, brick panels in
dazzling cabalistic patterns and a castellated
parapet. Severn Trent's story is that it houses
pumps to supply water from bore holes to Bilston.
Now who would believe that, when it is obviously
the secret lair of a fearsome giant, probably
Severn Trent's Chief Accountant.

The railway was built by the Great Western between 1912 and 1925 from the main line at Wolverhampton to Brierly Hill, near Dudley. It was closed in 1966 and converted to a walking, cycling route in the 1970's. You can go as far north as Tettenhall, Wolverhamton and south to the end at Fenns Pools. Wombourn Station is on the Walk and houses a small exhibition.

✳

THE STROLL
I like the strolls to be shorter than this 2 mile circuit, but short of walking you along roads, there is not much choice. You can obviously take a turn down the canal and back if you like.

✳

(1) From picnic site cross canal bridge. Join towpath & go DOWNSTREAM appx .6 mile, past bridges (1) & (2) to bridge (3) (flat concrete with pipe in front).

(2) Exit to lane & go L over canal to junction. Go L appx 60 yds & take path R by stream.

(3) Follow stream appx .6 mile to embankment & go up L to join railway.

(4) Follow appx .75 mile to old station, & exit R down to road.

(5) Go R appx 300 yds to start.

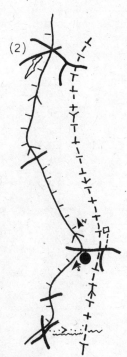

THE BRATCH

THE WALK
About 4 miles of canal and railway give a rewarding short walk in an otherwise rather featureless landscape.

After Bratch Locks is an windy and gently winding section of the canal to handsome Awbridge bridge, which has unusual slotted parapets. The cut continues more sheltered by hedges and trees. The railway is straight and serious and slightly downhill, rural, silent and fringed by wildflowers.

(1) From picnic site cross canal & go up past locks. Follow towpath appx 1.5 miles (past 3 locks) to Dimmingsdale Bridge by pond & glasshouses.

(2) Exit to road, cross bridge & take R fork. Go appx 500 yds (past lane R) to join railway. Go R 2.25 miles to old station.

(3) Exit L thro car park to road, & go R back to start.

BUSES run details 0785 223344

Castle Ring

WHERE
Map reference SK 045127, Landranger 128 Derby & Burton on Trent. An Iron Age hill fort on the southern tip of Cannock Chase just north of Hednesford. Buses run - details 0785 223344.

PARK & PICNIC
Park by the Ring, picnic anywhere, you have 26 square miles of Chase. The Park Gate pub is near.

THE PLACE
Castle Ring is the highest point on Cannock Chase at about 820 feet. The ramparts enclose 17 acres of rough grass where a community and animals could be safe. There is argument whether these Iron Age camps were permanently occupied or just fortifications used in dangerous times. Some have no water supply, but this one does. Go to the north edge and you can see miles across the sweep of the Chase. Thanks to the Forestry Commission for removing their Scots Pine which used to hide this view, because it brings the Ring to life. You can see the reason for it, a sound defensive position.

The Chase is a gravel and sand plateau of about 26 square miles standing clear from the green fields around, but cut in two by the deep valley between Rugeley and Cannock. Until 1550 there was dense oakwood, which by 1600 had been clear felled for charcoal to fuel local iron furnaces. Overgrazing by sheep followed and left an eroded moorland on thin acid soil. The northern part is generally open, the south forested. There are deer and the

Anson Pines planted in 1770 to commemorate Admiral Anson's circumnavigation of the earth, with some still standing. And here and there, like a distant bugle call, are remains of the Army training camp of Word War I. Go to the Visitor Centre at Marquis Drive to find out more.

THE STROLL
A 1.5 mile wander round the woods with a nice pool.

(1) From car park JUST enter Ring area, then go R along car park fence & join wood path.

(2) Cross grass ride & on to track. Go L to house & take track R just before it.

(3) Follow appx .3 mile down to pool L. Take track R appx .4 mile to cross roads.

(4) Take track up R by power poles to crest & junctions. Go L & join paths by Ring. ●

THE WALK
This 4 mile circuit is a fair sampling of the hills and woodland of the southern Chase. There are pools and lakes, cathedral tall stands of Scots and Corsican Pine and bright green spaces between the mature trees. Recent Forestry Commission felling has hugely improved the views on this walk, and you can see the panorama of dark and light greens over the steep hillsides from the high point of Castle Ring, and view the Ring itself from a distance.

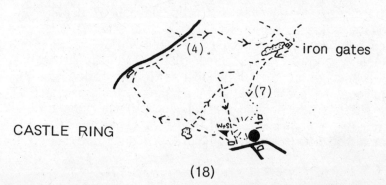

iron gates

CASTLE RING

Paras (1) & (2)
as the STROLL

(3) Follow appx 1.25 mile, past pool L, & on to house & road.

(4) Take path with road on your L appx .5 mile, cross 1st track, to 2nd with car park R.

(5) Take track forking away from road appx 1 mile, (cross track, round corkscrew bend) to T junction with pool opposite.

(6) Go R to wrought iron gates. Go R to fork by power pole. Take rising track ahead (not R) to its end.

(7) Take rising wood path ahead. As it becomes less clear, look for power poles & fence L & go parallel, going UP to summit & nearer to fence.

(8) When fence bends L, make for rampart of Ring & join, going L or R back to car park.●

Coughton Ford

WHERE
Map reference SP 085604, Landranger 150 Worcester & The Malverns. A ford across the River Arrow just west of the A435 at Coughton, north of ALCESTER. Buses run - details 0905 766802.

PARK & PICNIC
A car park with picnic tables by the river managed by the National Trust. Beware voracious ducks.

THE RIVER AND COUGHTON COURT.
The Arrow rises in Redditch and after its first mile or so has been joined by several little brooks to become a proper small river. It winds and curls south in a broad flat bottomed valley beside the north - south ridge on which the Romans built

Ryknild Street (A435 to us). After Coughton it
wiggles on through Alcester, where the River Alne
joins from the north east, then loops and bends
madly south into the Avon just west of Bidford.
There were once eight mills and a forge.

Coughton Court was started in the early 1500's and
the dominant feature is the gatehouse, completed
in 1509. The Estate came to the Throckmorton family
in 1409 and they have lived there ever since. This
is surprising because the Throckmortons were
indomitable Roman Catholics who suffered financial
penalties,loss of civil rights and imprisonment in
the religious upheavals between the 1530's and
1700. A potted history of the Court would include;

1583 Throckmorton Plot to kill Queen Elizabeth,
1605 Coughton Court used by the Gunpowder Plotters,
1643 occupied by Parliamentary troops,
1644 bombarded by Royalist artillery,
1688 sacked by a Protestant mob.

The National Trust acquired the Estate in 1949 with
the Throckmortons as tenants. Go and see the
paintings and priest holes, the shields and devices
round the door and the views from the tower.

THE STROLL
A peaceful 2 miles with a classic front view of
Coughton Court.

(1) From picnic site cross
bridge & follow lane to A435.

CAREFULL - TRAFFIC

(2) Take lane opposite, cross
old railway to next house R.

(3) Just past house take gate
R. Follow field edge to end,
then grass track L to farm.
Pass it & follow drive to lane.

(4) Go R, cross old railway &
just before 1st house L, take
fenced path L to stile & field.

(5) Go to bottom R corner &
take stile. Go with stream on
your L to A435.

CAREFULL

(6) Cross & go R to take white
iron kissing gate L. Go
straight to church & drive. Go
R to lane then L back to ford.

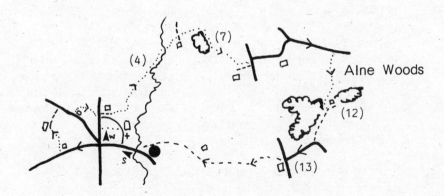

COUGHTON FORD

THE WALK

About 5.5 miles with a grassy walk up the Arrow Valley and past some of the river's contortions, then a climb into the Alne Hills at about 360 feet. There are wide views of hilly woodland misting into the distance, and the way back is an exhilarating roll down farm tracks. In wet weather you will meet some mud on the return track; nothing sensational.

✱

(1) From picnic site cross river & follow lane to A435. Go R to cross river bridge & at cottages take track R.

(2) Cross stile, cross field diagonally & take corner stile. Take (or bypass) two stiles & cross next stile.

(3) Go L along hedge, round field corner, & take gate L. Cross field diagonally, to R side of tree clump with farm beyond, & take double barred stiles.

(4) Follow river & cross bridge. Bear R & take small red gate just L of farm house.

(5) Go L a few paces & after barn, go R in field parallel with R hedge, & take end gate.

(6) Go with hedge on your R & take corner stile. Go R up wood edge to end & cross stile. ◢

(7) Sight trees below & cross field to take hedge gap L of them. Sight trees above L & head for their R end, entering via gap opposite power pole.

(8) Exit via stile. Go L along wood edge & take gate to lane.

(9) Take lane opposite, thro farm, to T junction. Go R appx 700 yds up to CREST (with cottage 75 yds ahead & gate L). Take ramp R to gate & field.

(10) Go with hedge on your L to next field, continue & take corner gate.

(11) Pass track L & follow track ahead, up thro new wood to take stile. Follow edge of wood on R to track by sheds L.

(12) Go down R to lane. Go R to T junction.

(13) Go R a few paces & cross lane to take track R of house. Follow appx 1.3 miles to start.

WHERE

Map reference SP 463692, Landranger 140 Leicester & Coventry. A Severn Trent reservoir with Warwickshire County Council's Country Park beside it. Two miles south of DUNCHURCH on the A426. Buses run to Dunchurch - details 0926 412135.

PARK & PICNIC

Parking (60p per car) and picnic space with WC's.

THE PLACE

The Country Park is on the delightful green Hensborough Hill, only 330 feet high but giving wide views over the reservoir and the flat valley of the River Leam.

Draycote Water was built in 1964 to serve Rugby, is about 2.5 miles around and covers 600 acres. You can sail, surfboard and fish. You can also walk the shore or watch birds, but you need a permit costing £4 per year per person. Is this something to do with the permissive society?

Opened by Transport Minister Ernest Marples in the early 1960's, the M45 is now our only decent Motorway. Remember, the London - Birmingham route (M1 and M45) on which you never had to stop for traffic lights, roundabouts, bikes or prams. Here excited radiators boiled, and exhausted conrods, cranks, big ends, fan belts and clutches ground, bust, split and shattered at their first experience of going faster that 30 miles an hour for twenty minutes without a rest. Now just a

forgotten limb of the M1 waving vaugely towards
Coventry, it is comfortable, rural, a bumbly
Beeching branch, where you can wave to the canal
boats and the cows.

THE STROLL
There is no short walk from the picnic site except
to wander down to the lake shore and on for half a
mile to a cattle grid. Here is a grim sign telling
you that you are not wanted beyond. However the
return trip from the park entrance is about 1.5
miles, if this will do. Below is a short walk which
can be done with the main walk or separately, of
about 2.2 miles.

THE WALK(S)
There is no sensible walk which you can start from
the Country Park without lots of road. To start
this one you must travel the short distance to the
M45 bridge at Dunchurch.

The first section (A) of this 5.5 mile route can be
cut off to give a Stroll of 2.2 miles, or you can
just do the other 3.3 miles (B). However the
detachable section is arguable the best.

After a walk beside the reservoir (from which you
are carefully fenced off) you enter a landscape of
level fields and dense high hedges of hawthorne,
hazel and blackthorn. There are fine views from the
hill on which Dunchurch stands. Watch out for the
splendid pocket sewage works. Sadly it will soon be
screened from view by the paranoid secrecy of
Severn Trent, who are trying to shroud it in trees.

✱

(1) From Dunchurch, cross M45, go 100 yds to post box & take lane R.

(2) Follow & take path L just before 1st house L, to driveway

(3) Bear R a few paces & take stile opposite to field. Go down midfield dip & take gate to track.

****
MIDDLE WALK (B)
Go L 50yds; face plank bridge L
NEXT Para (7)
****

(4) Take gate opposite & go with hedge on your L 3 fields to take gate L.

(5) Pass farm on your R, join track & on to lane. Go ahead to R bend by church.◀

(6) Take gate L & down concrete track to take stile. Follow fenced path (if obstructed by growth or insects use field) to stile & track.

****
SHORT WALK (A)
(6a) Go L a few paces & take gate R, then up midfield & take stile to drive.

(6b) Go R a few paces & curve L to take corner gate. Follow path to lane & R back to start.●
****

(7) Cross track & take plank bridge & stile. Go R along fence via stiles (1) & (2) to fenced path.

(8) Follow up to stile & hedged track. Go R to its end.▶

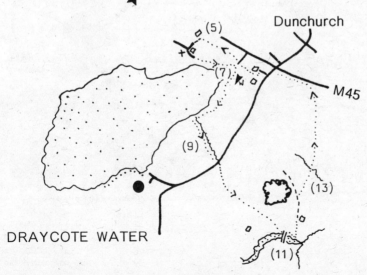

Dunchurch

(5)

(7)

M45

(9)

(13)

DRAYCOTE WATER

(11)

(9) Go R along fence, pass works & cross stream then stile to open field. Go L with stream on your L, via gates, to A426.

(10) Go L a few paces & take hedge gap opposite to field. Go with hedges on your L appx .8 mile. After farm at far R, go 2 fields to gate & stream ahead.

(11) Go L & take stile, then R, past steel bridge & round field corner, to farm track. ◢

(12) Go L & count to 5th power pole (No.31). Take green track R, curving L to projecting hedge, then with hedge on your L to stile.

(13) Go with hedges on your L to end of green track by red shed, & follow it to field end.

(14) Go L on field edge track to A426 & M45 bridge. ●

Forehill

WHERE
Map reference SP 056755, Landranger 139 Birmingham.
A high point on a cross roads. (From M42 JUNCTION 3
(A435), take A435 (Birmingham) to next roundabout.
Take first exit left for a mile, pass first road
left and take second left on bend.) There is a pub
and WC's, which are usually closed but I expect
Hereford & Worcester County Council have a jolly
good reason. Bus details 0905 766802.

THE PLACE
Unlike most of the other picnic places, Forhill is
not a great beauty spot and has no exiting history.
Hereford & Worcester County Council just seem to
have had a bit of land left from a road scheme. But
it is very pleasant, quite high at nearly 600 feet,
and there is a nice little pub. There are no
striking views from the site because the hills in
this part of north Worcestershire are great broad
backed domes. A sleepy landscape of hedges, deep
ponds in clay hollows and red brick farms.

The Forhill site lies on a that famous short Long
Distance Footpath, the North Worcestershire Path.
In the late 1970's the County Council decided to
link their Country Parks in the north of the
county. The 30 mile route starts at Kingsford on
the southern end of Kinver Edge and visits the
Clent Hills, the Waseley Hills and Lickey Hills, It
was later extended to Forehill, then to Majors
Green on the Solihull boundary. The path is
maintained with the help of the City of Birmingham
Group of the Ramblers Association.

(27)

THE STROLL

About 2 miles with a drop and a climb of 200 feet.
This is lovely sweeping rolling country. See the
view back, through and over the trees as you climb
the last section. A welly walk in wet weather.

*

(1) Leave picnic site, take lane on R of pub appx 300 yds & take stile L on wood corner.

(2) Go thro to stile & field, then down parallel with lane R. Keep same line via stiles to stile on R of house, & lane.

(3) Take lane opposite appx 150 yds, then stile R. Go with hedge on your R & take field corner stile.◀

(4) Keep same line & take field end stile. Bear R with stream & take stile. Go ahead, curving L to stile & lane.

(5) Take stile opposite. Go parallel with stream L & take L corner stile. Go up hedge & take top L field corner stile.

(6) Go R up field edge, cross 2 stiles, then L to stile & lane. Go R to T junction & L to picnic site.●

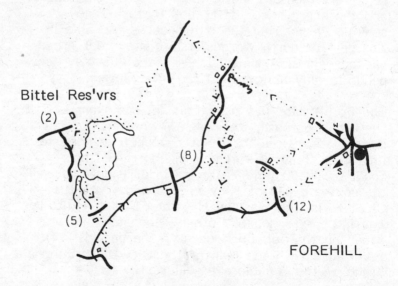

Bittel Res'vrs

(2)

(8)

(5)

(12)

FOREHILL

THE WALK(S)

About 7.5 miles (Route A) with an alternative of 4.25 miles (Route B).

A varied walk with woods and ponds, the Bittell Reservoirs which feed the Worcester & Birmingham Canal, and the canal through the woody, muddy Hopwood Cutting. The canal was completed in 1815 to provide a direct route to the Severn. There is not much water on the Birmingham plateau and 10 reservoirs were built to feed the 58 locks.

Route (B) follows the canal past the mouth of the 2726 yard Wast Hill Tunnel, sunk deep in a shrubby cutting. The towpath is a bit submersible and a welly walk, so there is an alternative.

✱

(1) Leave picnic site, take lane on R side of pub & next lane R. Pass 2 houses L & take next stile R.

[Next 3.5 miles clearly marked "North Worcs Path". Note these points as you pass so that you know when to leave it.]

   * circle farm
   * deep pond L & sloping lane
   * wood, field edge & lane.

** Route B next para (1a)**

   * by sports field
   * deep dingle
   * main road
   * covert
   * fields ▲

* lake side
* field edges
* farm drive meets lane

(2) Where farm drive meets lane with white signs, go L to end of 2nd pond at sharp R bend.

(3) Take stile L to dam, go R to end & take stile R.

(4) Go up with fence on your L, take stile & follow grass track to stile & lane.

(5) Enter farm opposite. Pass pond L, take gate R & go L down track to cross canal.

(6) Take stile R. Sight white & red houses & go appx 100yds L of them to corner stile & road. ➤

►(7) Go R to bridge & join towpath. Go R (UPSTREAM) appx 1.5 miles:

* pass warning sign, route a bit prickly but OK if you use banktop path

* pass under A441 by pub, go on to next bridge & take stile R.

►(8) Go with hedge on your R to field corner & take gate R.

►(9) Follow hedge on your L & take corner stile. Keep same line to join stream. Take stile to cross fence AND stream.

(10) Go L by stream & take stile, then half R to projecting hedge corner & take gate. Go with hedge on your L to gate & lane.

(11) Go L appx .6 mile to T junction.

(12) Take stile L of house. Go parallel with R hedge & take stile. Keep same line via stiles (then with lane on your L) thro small wood to lane.

(13) Go R to picnic site. ●

****
Route B

(1a) Go L on lane, pass big house gate R & take stile R to field. Cross & take gateway in opposite hedge.

(1b) Go L along hedge & take corner stile. Cross midfield to bottom R corner & take stile just L of house, to lane.

****
Towpath is welly job; alternative - para (1bi) below
****

(1c) Go R, pass house & take path R to canal.

(1d) Follow towpath (or bank top alternative) to pass under 2nd bridge & take stile L.

now Route (A) para (8) ◄

****
** alternative **

(1bi) Cross lane & take stile. Sight bottom midfield oak; head for it then past it (above hollow) to stile & lane.

(1bii) Take gate opposite, make for power pole ahead & take corner stile. Bear half L & take field corner gate.

now Route (A) para (9)◄
****

Habberley Valley

WHERE
Map reference SO 802776, Landranger 138, Kidder-
-minster & Wyre Forest. A valley at the end of a
track off the B4190 Bewdley - Wolverley road. Buses
run - details 0562 829400.

PARK & PICNIC
Cars use the middle of the large grass area but
recent purchase of the Valley by the District
Council may result in more specific arrangements.
Pincic anywhere.

THE VALLEY
On 1st December 1991 Wyre Forest District Council
bought the Valley as a public open space. There
will be a visitor centre and information leaflets
on the flora and fauna, history and geology.

The 60 acre valley area is a curved wall of triasic
(Old Red) sandstone with softer greyish sand at its
foot, and the red crag of Peckett Rock as an
outcrop in this arena. It seems to have been
naturally formed and there is no evidence of
quarrying, though common sense suggests that it
must have occurred in some places. Long ago an
arm of the sea extended from the Bristol Channel to
cover much of the Severn plain, and Habbereley
Valley was a bay on its shores. As the sea
retreated it became a backwater, then a saltmarsh.
There is the fascinating evidence of several
maritime plants including a grey haired grass.

The Valley has been a resting, courting and holiday
spot for Kidderminster weavers and Black Country
workers. It has worn well and remains about the
best area of heather heathland in the County.

THE STROLL
About 1 mile. Just wander up the valley (passing
the big white house on your left) by any of the
paths or tracks that you please. You can come back
by several parallel routes.

There are three ways up the rock wall at the valley
head and very fine views from the top. The first is
easy and you can find it by going behind the big
solitary Pecket Rock and probing in that corner.
Another way, but very steep, is from the opposite
side of the valley head. The third route is part of
the Walk.

THE WALK
About 5 miles, with delightful paths through
woodland, four ponds and sandy tracks winding
beside rocky cliffs. From a summit at about 500
feet there are views of the Abberley Hills and the
Clees to the west, and as you turn east, a
panorama, with wooded Kinver Edge and nearby hills,
the Clent Hills with the cocks crest of beeches on
Adams Hill, and Wychbury with its monument.

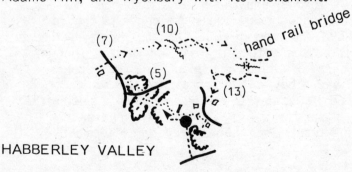

HABBERLEY VALLEY

✳

(1) From centre of valley take track to L of big white house. At fork go R (by big house garden) to fence corner R.

(2) Go with fence on your L. At fork follow main path. After steps, see red house ahead & bear L. Go up to meet path, then R to take stile.

(3) Cross midfield & take stile, then thro wood to track. Go R to lane.

(4) Cross bearing R & take track opposite, round R curve & enter wood.

(5) Go up parallel with wood edge on R (central path a little L is OK), to meet lane.

(6) Go R, pass Trimpley Green Farm L & track R, to next farm track L by pond.

(7) Take path R opposite farm, if prickly find clear path a few paces on, & take stile.

(8) Go with hedge on your R & take stile. Cross midfield heading L of centre of row of oaks, & take stile.

(9) Head for midfield trees ahead & take gate to their R. Follow ridge type path to take bottom field corner stile.

(10) Go with stream on your R & take stile to track. Go R to R bend & take stile L.

(11) Follow valley path .5 mile, past bridge (1) R, & take single handrail bridge (2) R.

(12) Go ahead & via 3 stiles to track. Go R .4 mile to meet wide track.

(13) Go L to lane. Go L to L bend & junction. Go ahead appx 100 yds & take steep path R down to valley.

(33)

Hampton in Arden

WHERE
Map reference SP 213282, Landranger 139 Birmingham.
A old bridge over the River Blythe by the railway
about a mile south of Hampton in Arden. No buses
but there are trains from Birmingham and Coventry.

PARK & PICNIC
There are parking spaces. Hampton in Arden Parish
Council's picnic area was a bit rudimentary when I
called, but you should find space in the area.

THE PLACE
A narrow grey stone packhorse bridge crosses the
little River Blythe, which writhes through a reedy,
weedy landscape. Gaze down into the water, it is
surprisingly clear. Dwarfing but not diminishing
this bridge is the vast blue brick railway viaduct.
This is the main Birmingham - London line. Wave if
you like, but modern trains are too busy to wave
back. The chain of pools to the south were left
after gravel extraction.

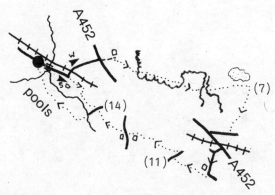

THE STROLL
A 1.5 mile amble passing the lakes. Wear wellies in wet weather.

✳

(1) From car park go with railway on your L, cross bridge, to bend with tunnel L.

(2) Take track ahead to bend, then L corner stile. Go with hedge on your L for 2 fields.

(3) Go R round field corner & take next corner stile L. Go 2 fields to stile & lane. ◢

(4) Go R, cross river & follow track to fork. Go R & follow sandy track with lakes on your L to end hedge.

(5) Round L bend, go to power pole & take bridge R. Follow path to start. ●

THE WALK
About 6 miles with a pine wood, parkland, some lakes and an excursion to see Berkeswell Church.

✳

(1) From car park go with railway on your L, cross bridge to bend then L to A452.

TRAFFIC - VERY GREAT CARE

(2) Take lane opposite to farm. Enter 1st gate & take stile R.

(3) Go diagonally L, join R hedge at gateway & go with hedge on your R to wood.

(4) Follow path down wood edge, then with hedge on your L 2 fields. Cross corner of wood to stile & big field. ◢

(5) Path usually clear. If not, look along line of R hedge to 1st oak & take a line appx 15 yds L of it. Cross midfield to stile & enter wood corner.

(6) Follow path thro wood to kissing gate & track by bridge.

TO VISIT BERKESWELL
cross track & take path
across causeway to church.

(7) Go R on field path & with fence on your R to lane. Go R to A452.

TRAFFIC - CARE ▶

(8) Cross & go L over railway. Enter lane R, then take lane L, to bend by gates.

(9) Enter gates & at R bend take gate R of pond. Go R 2 fields to field corner.

(10) Cross gate then stile ahead, & go with hedge on your L to lane.

(11) Go R, pass gateway L & take stile L. Sight big skyline trees; go to L end & take stile.

(12) Go with hedge on your L to farm, & via stiles round R side to see gabled house ahead. Bear L & take barn end stile to track. Go R to lane.

(13) Enter drive opposite & take 2 stiles R. Cross field diagonally, pass L of sheds, & with hedge on your L to lane.

(14) Go R, cross river & follow track to fork. Go R & follow sandy track with lakes on your L to end hedge.

(15) Round L bend, go to power pole & take bridge R. Follow path to start.

Hartlebury Common

WHERE
Map reference SO 827714, Landranger 138 Kidder-
-minster & Wyre Forest. Heathland between
Stourport and Hartlebury on the B4193. Buses run -
details 0562 829400.

PARK & PICNIC
Parking space with picnic tables.

THE COMMON
This 215 acres of dry sandy heathland was
designated an SSSI in 1955 and has been managed
(and is now owned) by the County Council since
1957. They publish leaflets on the structure, flora
and fauna and management of the Common which you
can get from libraries and tourist offices.

Lowland heath is an unusual habitat in the
Midlands, the other main example is Cannock Chase.
The heath was shaped by the River Severn, now 140
feet below, as a series of gravel terraces.
Windblown sand accumulated and was stabilised by
plants, gorse and broom on the upper plateau level
and heather on the lower terrace. A boggy area in
the lower terrace provides habitat for another
range of plants and creatures.

You may find Shepherds Cress, Sheeps Sorrel,
Buckshorn Plantain and Heath Bedstraw, with Bog
Bean, Cotton Grass and Moss Cinquefoil in the
boggy bit. There are lizards, grass snakes, weasels
and rabbits, whinchats and stonechats and over 100
varieties of butterflies and moths.

In the past grazing animals and rabbits maintained
the heathland, but following myximatosis in the
1950's, scrub and trees grew and spread, shading
out and dominating smaller and less common plants.
The management policy is to reduce and control the
trees, bigger shrubby plants and the bracken,
broom and gorse. Left to itself, nature would have
a dense wood on Hartlebury Common, so the County
are trying to stop the clock at the heathland phase
of landscape development.

*

STROLL & SLIGHTLY LONGER STROLL
The steep sandy hills, sandstone cliffs and small
wooded valleys once formed a gorgeous landscape
around Stourport and the Common. Now the land not
covered by cabbage and beet fields and punctuated
by pylons, is littered with ill planned housing
and small factories. This tacky corner is nobody's
fault and everybody's, and the clearest possible
case for planning control.

There are (in my view) no attractive circular walks
which are clear of obstructions that you can reach
from the Common, but there are a couple of very
enjoyable wanders on the Common itself, (A) is 1.25
miles and (B) 2.5 miles.

You meet a stream that has become a marsh, with
willows and coppiced hazel up to their stools in
water. Further on is a chain of clear ponds edged
with tall grasses and a forest of bullrushes.

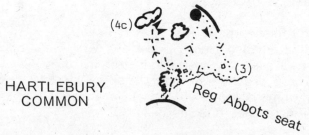

(4c)

(3)

HARTLEBURY
COMMON

Reg Abbots seat

(A) SHORT STROLL

(1) Face car park side of information board. Go L across track & pass white concrete trig point R to take stile.

(2) Go down with hedge on your R, pass under power lines & take stile R by pylon.

(3) Follow lower field edge & take STILE (not gate). Go with fence on your R to pass shed & pools to "Reg Abbotts" seat.

(4) Pass seat a few paces & take path up R to farm & lane.

(5) Bear R past farm & follow heath edge path (with fence on your R) back to car park. ●

(B) LONGER STROLL

Follow SHORT STROLL to para (4)

(4a) Take sandy horse track just R of information board & follow, curving R, appx 200 yds to x tracks.

(4b) Go L & again curve up R, to meet track on crest with small wood ahead.

(4c) Face wood & look R, the far wood you now see is in direction of car park.

OPTIONS

(i) follow horse track towards distant wood OR

(ii) enter nearby wood to gain edge of scarp & make your way along it OR

(iii) go down scarp to lower terrace and follow tracks R.

(4d) Car park is on highest point at north end of scarp. Approaching car park there are three houses beyond. ●

Hartshill Hayes

WHERE
Map reference SP 306941, Landranger 140 Leicester &
Coventry. A Warwickshire County Council site
between Nuneaton and Atherstone. There is a second
picnic site at Oldbury Cutting .75 mile away and
signposted. Buses run - details 0926 42135.

PARK & PICNIC
At Hartshill you pay 70p for your car and get loos
and a Visitor Centre. The Stroll and the Walk start
from Oldbury, which is free.

THE PLACE
Nuneaton is a mining town with the usual pitheaps
and mess, but like many mining districts, on its
doorstep is some glorious countryside. The slag
heaps have largely been landscaped and clothed with
green. The ridge of which Hartshill Hayes is part
runs north east from Nuneaton and reaches some 500
feet. This is not alpine , but it towers over the
plain which vanishes mistly into the far east, and
gives amazing views.

There are many oak and beech woods, the Coventry
Canal, a burial mound and the ruins of a castle. Go
to the Visitor Centre and find out more.

THE STROLL
A 3 mile wander with wide exhilarating views of a
chequerboard landscape from the Hayes, two
contrasting woods, and a chance to have a nosey
peer into peoples' gardens.

*

(1) From Oldbury Cutting Car Park, go down grass picnic area to end, & take 2 stiles.

(2) Follow old railway & take next stile, then on 50 yds & take stile L.

(3) Go with hedge on your R via 2 stiles, then ahead midfield to join hedge corner.

(4) Go with hedge on your L, round field corner, & take 1st stile L. Cross field corner & take stile.

(5) Bear L (past quarry R) & follow fenced track, then R on fenced path & take stile.

(6) Go up to crest, heading just R of multi chimnied red roof, & take stile to lane. Take track opposite to Park.

(7) Bear R & follow steel fence R to wood corner. Continue on path to Visitor Centre.

(8) Pass it on your L & approach Park entrance. Appx 10yds before gate, take stile L

(10) Follow wood path parallel with road R. At each fork go R, pass 1st entrance R to 2nd, & exit to road. ◀

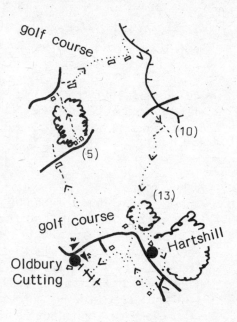

HARTSHILL HAYES

(11) Go L & take 1st road R. Pass Hill St R, pass grass triangle L & take Moorwood Cresc R. Pass road R to L bend.

(12) Take track opposite. Cross a track & bend R, past houses, to last house (L).

(13) Take stile & rising track (NOT PATH L), cross a track & bend L into wood. Follow straight path & take end stile.

(14) Keep same line with fence on your R, & via stiles & fenced path to quarry.

(15) Bear L & take corner stile. ▶

(41)

[I expect you can find your way back, but the rest is in anyway for the Walkers]

►(16) Cross field corner & take stile. Go R on field edge & round corner to hedge end. ◄

(17) Go ahead midfield to projecting hedge corner, then with hedge on your L via stiles to embankment.

(18) Go R & keep same line back to start. ●

THE WALK

About 5.5 miles with some 250 feet between the summit on Hartshill and the bottom at the Coventry Canal. This is one of the most varied walks in the books and a revelation to anyone who thought that the country round Nuneaton was drab. Actually, to the east of Harsthill Hayes, there are miles upon flat miles stretching across Leicestershire. But the glory of this place is that you have it at your feet, and all around are pretty woods on hilly slopes. On this walk you cross two golf courses, walk a winding canal and pass through a wood of rhodedendrons with interesting boggy patches.

＊

(1) Leave Oldbury Cutting car park & go R on lane appx 500yds to Moorwood Farm R.

(2) Go on a few paces & take hedge gap L to golf course. Aim for farm on horizon ahead;

> Go ahead & pass golf tee (hump & yellow knobs) on your R, cross fairway & bear L to pass next tee on your R

> Keep same line & cross green, then next tee on your R, & with bushes on your R to hedge gap & field.

(3) Follow clear midfield path, then with hedge on your R, & via farm drive to lane.

(4) Go R appx 400 yds, past 2 houses L & Z bend sign. Go a few paces on & take path L by red brick wall.

(5) Follow to end of wall, then take track ahead appx .5 mile, past house to lane.

(6) Go R to next L bend. Take track R to its end, then stile to golf course.

(7) Bear L around green ahead, then R to join hedge path. Go with hedge on your R .5 mile, past club house R, to house R. Bear L on track to canal. ◢

(8) Cross bridge & take towpath R. Pass under 1st bridge to 2nd (double) one & exit L to lane.

(9) Cross canal & go appx 50 yds to take track L. Follow appx 400 yds & take track R.

(10) Follow to its end, then keep same line across field corner & join rising hedge.

(11) Go with hedge on your R over crest, then down on fenced path to field corner.

(12) Go L on fenced path & take gate, then with hedge on your L, round field corner to wood.

(13) Follow rising wood path to top, then up with trees on your R to crest.

[For Visitor Centre etc follow steel fence to L]

(14) Bear R to end of steel fence & take track to lane. Take stile opposite.

(15) Go down midfield & take stile to fenced path. Go R to end, then L on track to pass quarry L, & take corner stile.

next - STROLL para (16) ▶

(43)

Highgate Common

WHERE
Map reference SO 835900, Landranger 138 Kidder-
-minster & Wyre Forest. A sandy heath south west
of Wolverhampton just off the B4176 (Wombourne -
Bridgnorth) road. Buses run - details 0785 223344.

PARK & PICNIC
Highgate Common is managed by Staffordshire County
Council and has eight car parks around its edge.
There are acres for picnics within reach of each
one. The SUPER STROLL is a circular tour of the
whole area and passes all the parks. You can start
at any of them.

THE COMMON
The 278 acres of Highgate Common is one of the few
areas of lowland heath left in the Midlands, others
are Cannock Chase, Habberley Valley and Hartlebury
Common. Like them and much of the land to the west
of the West Midlands area, the ground is fine and
sandy and in places forms thin acid soils. During
World War II Highgate was cleared of trees and an
attempt made to farm it. No doubt it grew
something, heaven knows at what cost, but that was
abandoned in 1949 and the heath recolonised by
birch. Now we have heathers, bilberry, bracken and
wavy hair grass. There is beech in the south,
Corsican Pine in the enclosed Forestry area (a seed
orchard), Lodgepole pine in the middle and oak
swathed in honeysuckle to the north, with birch
everywhere. Take time to ponder some of the small
ponds, some of which are quite recent, since
someone discovered a new purpose for Boy Scouts.

SUPER STROLL

There is gorgeous countryside within a couple of miles of Highgate, but the immediate landscape is flat and arable, hence the nearby airfield. To get to the good stuff would involve a longer walk than normal, and a lot of it unrewarding.

You can stroll and wander as you like over the common, and you don't need me for that. Also, the County Council publish a leaflet (20p) with waymarked walks. My contribution is a 4 mile circuit of the boundary for a full appreciation of the Common in all its variety, and for those who like to "do" a place sytematically.

The car parks appear in clockwise order. I have started at New Lodge for no special reason, you can start at any of them. There are obvious shortcuts, or you could wander about at will till you found a car park, then use the notes to get back to base.

NEW LODGE CAR PARK

(1) Put your back to entrance track & take R of 2 paths.

(2) Go parallel with boundary R appx .4 mile to 2 wooden barriers L & horseshoe post R.

(3) Go L thro barriers & FOLLOW WOOD EDGE via right angle corners appx 1.25 miles, to signpost (Staffs Way - Public Bridleway) by gate R.

(4) Go L by conifers to road. Cross & continue. Within sight of road ahead, path bends L to

MAJORS CAR PARK.

(5) Put park entrance on your R & go ahead appx 200 yds to

POOL CAR PARK.

(6) Put park entrance on your R & face line of trees. Head for L end of conifers, enter gap & take path up, with birches & fence on your L.

(7) When fence turns L, keep same line along power poles to

CAMP HILL ROAD CAR PARK.

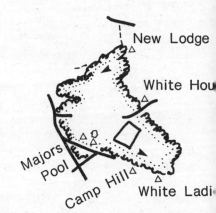

(8) Put park entrance on your R & follow power poles to

WHITE LADIES CAR PARK.

(9) Put your back to park entrance & go to far end. Take R of 3 paths, curving R to pass fence corner R. Go with fence on your R to next corner (iron farm shed in view).

(10) Go L, parallel with boundary fence R, appx .5 mile via right angle bend, to lane &

WHITE HOUSE CAR PARK.

(11) Enter park from lane & go to far end. Go parallel with boundary fence R .6 mile to

NEW LODGE CAR PARK.

Kingsbury Water Park

WHERE
Map reference SP 203960, Landranger 139 Birmingham.
Lakes near Kingsbury on the B4097 from Birmingham.

Buses run - details 0926 412929. From the church
bus stop, take the path past the church and down to
cross the footbridge over the River Tame. This puts
you on the far side of the park from the Visitor
Centre and car park, and at para (10) of the Walk.

PARK & PICNIC
Free entry but cars pay £1 each. The Water Park
closes to vehicles at dusk but you can still get
out. For times and information phone 0827 872660.

THE WATER PARK
By 1973 some 50 years of gravel working had left
this 600 acre section of the Tame valley a series
of pits separated by narrow necks of ground. Some
had already been filled with fly ash from Hams
Hall Power Station, but most had brimmed naturally
with water. Warwickshire County Council encouraged
natural colonisation by mosses, grasses, reeds,
willows, brambles, birch and oak, they added to it
with new planting and laid some tracks and paths.
There are now 30 lakes and pools. You can walk
round many of the secluded fishing pools in a
couple of minutes, but Bodymoor Heath Water is 66
acres, Hemlingford Water only a little smaller and
Cliff Pool, Canal Pool, Broomeycroft Pool, Mill
Pool and Swann Pool and all proper lakes.

(47)

You can do all sorts of things at Kingsbury Water
Park - sail, windsurf, fish, orienteer, go mad in a
power boat, ride horses, camp or caravan, sail
model boats, or walk. Get a leaflet and find out.

SUPER STROLL
The Water Park is fascinating but the surrounding
landscape is the wide, wet bottom of the Tame
Valley, part of industrial working Warwickshire
with few footpaths. There is no scenic walk nearby
but here is a 4.5 mile tour of the Park.

The County Council have laid out short walks, with
information leaflets and waymarked posts all over
the place. There is Phil Drabble's Nature Trail and
there are Spring, Summer, Autumn and Winter Walks
which you can get from the Visitor Centre.

✳

(1) Leaving Visitor Centre go L past cafe & take path to lane.

(2) Take path ahead 30 yds, go L past car park & cross bridge.

(3) Go on a few paces, turn L across lane & take path opposite .5 mile to meet track.

(4) Go L under M42 & on 200 yds to track junction. Go R to junction, then L to grass area.

(5) Go down grass with pool on your R to pool corner. Go L to stile & lane.

(6) Go R to canal. Take towpath R past lock, then follow raised track to end of pools & gate.

(7) Take path R, pass bird hides, pass two paths R & one L to bridge L.

(8) Cross bridge then take path L, pass path R & go up to M42.◀

(9) Go R on paths parallel with M42 to meet track. Go L; at fork by post >6 go R to >7.

(10) Go L to field, then R by trees to sports field. Cross to brick bridge, DON'T TAKE IT.

(11) Go with river on your L on parallel path to next bridge.

(12) Take lane R, pass surfing club R, to junction.

(13) Go R & round L bend, pass houses far L, round R bend a few paces & take path L.

(14) Follow path PAST bridge R AND stile L & go immediately L.

(15) Follow path to meet track, go ahead to end & join lane.

(16) Bear L across grass & parallel with lane back to Visitor Centre. ●

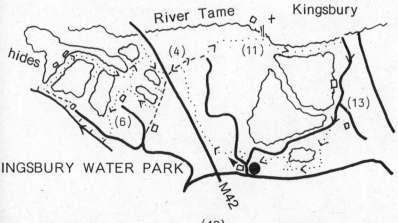

River Tame   Kingsbury

hides

(4)   7   (11)

(6)

(13)

INGSBURY WATER PARK

M42

Kingswood Common

WHERE
Map reference SJ 835029, Landranger 127 Stafford & Telford. A small wooded area on the A41 north of Wolverhampton. Bus details - 0785 223344.

PARK & PICNIC
There is a car park, some picnic tables from South Staffs District Council and lots of grass to sit on

THE PLACE
Common land belonged to a Lord of the Manor but the occupiers of nearby land had certain rights over it, such as collecting firewood or grazing.
Kingswood is a very small one compared with the others in the book, Pound Green, Yarningdale, Hartlebury and Highgate. The Commoners rights may well still exist, and at Pound Green they are excercised, but most commons are now simply public open spaces and many belong to local Councils. Oaken Lawn is a narow half mile long strip of land to the north east which features in both the Stroll and the Walk. This is also a common.

THE STROLL
There is no short circular which does not use too much road. This 2 mile wander is therefore a "there & back" by the same paths to visit the quiet and attractive Oaken Lawn. Welly walk.

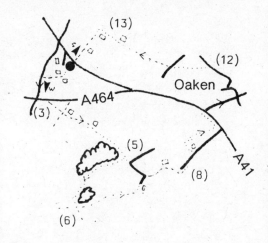

KINGSWOOD COMMON

✳

(1) Put car park entrance on your L & go parallel with road appx 100 yds. Go to road & cross into drive of Park Farm.

(2) Follow drive via stiles to its end & take L corner stile. Keep same line down field edge to take gate/stile.

(3) Go R down hedge & take gate/stile to track. Follow on same line appx .6 mile to road.

NOW RETURN ●

THE WALK

Six miles of level landscape with contrasting types of farming and views of the Wrekin and Brown Clee. (So someone said, it was driving sleet on the day I went.) The first half is busy modern arable farming with orchards, the second quiet grassland. You walk a section of the Staffordshire Way, meet a polite and lifeless Queen Anne style country house, a wood, a pretty village, and the curious narrow common of Oaken Lawn. Mud in places.

✳

(1) From car park entrance go to far R corner of common (lane on R side ends short of corner) to see buildings over hedge, & take track R to lane.

(2) Go L to A464, then L on pavement appx 100 yds. Cross & take path in hedge.

(3) Follow appx .5 mile; cross lane, becomes track, past house L, & down to steel gate. ◢

(4) Keep same line via small wooden gate & with wood on R to roads & wood corner.

(5) Go R on field edge with WOOD & FENCE ON YOUR R. Wood ends, keep on to corner of next wood. Bear R & follow R edge of wood, to track. ►

(51)

(6) Take track L appx .5 mile to iron shed. Take track down L side of shed to join drive, & go ahead to T junction.

(7) Go R a few paces & take track L to end. Bear R on track with beech hedge on your L.

(8) Pass front of house & bear R with hedge again, to its corner. Go appx 20 yds & take stile L onto drive.

(9) Go R to end. Go L & pass L corner of timber club house. Follow Staffs Way signs to pass brick shed L & on to power pole

(10) Go R on wood path, curves L to stile & field. Go R on field edge to corner, then with wall on your R to stile & A41.

(11) Take lane opposite appx .3 mile, then lane L. Road bears L to fork, go R. Pass FP signs R & last house (R), to R bend with gate & stile ahead.

(12) Take stile & go with hedge on your L to stile & lane. Take track opposite appx .6 mile & keep same line to track end at gate/stile.

(13) Take stile & go with hedge on your L to take stile L. Go with hedge on your R to join track. Pass farm to A41 & cross to Common.

Kingswood Junction

WHERE
Map reference SP 186710, Landranger 139 Birmingham.
The junction of two canals just west of the railway
at Lapworth on the B4439. No buses.

PARK & PICNIC
A signposted canalside parking and picnic area with
WC's (usually locked).

CANALS
Kingswood Junction is where the Stratford on Avon
and the Grand Union Canals pass and are linked by
a spur. There is a keepers cottage, a basin with
feeder pools, locks in three directions and a
handsome iron turnover bridge.

After 5 miles winding through Birmingham suburbs,
the Stratford Canal enters mild green Warwickshire
and heads south to Stratford and the Avon. With 55
locks, little white drawbridges and curious humped
roofed cottages, it wanders through small hills, a
romantic sleepy canal of brown cows and wild roses.
Without commercial traffic since the 1930's, it was
badly silted by the 1950's but rescued by the
National Trust in the 1960's.

The Grand Union Canal was completed in 1812 to link
Birmingham, London, Leicester and Nottingham. This
section comes from Birmingham via Solihull past
Kingswood Junction to Hatton Locks and Warwick.
The GU is not so much a poet's canal as an
accountant's, businesslike, but with crooked bits.

THE STROLL

Here are three alternatives
(A) Stratford Canal & green lane   (1.25 miles)
(B) Grand Union Canal & green lane   (2.5 miles)
(C) Grand Union & Stratford canals   (2.3 miles)

In damp weather the green lane is a welly job.

✳

(ALL START)
From picnic site get onto towpath. Go R to junction & cross bridge.

Route (A)
(A1) Take R canal past 5 locks to bridge.

(A2) Go R on track to junction. Go R, thro farm, to lane by picnic site. ●

Route (B)
(B1) Take canal L to junction. Go R to 2nd (road) bridge.

(B2) Get onto road facing pub & go L. Take 1st lane R & cross railway to canal bridge.

(B3) Continue on track up to junction. Go R, thro farm, to lane by picnic site. ●

Route (C)
Follow (B1) & (B2).

(C1) Go R on canal to start. ●

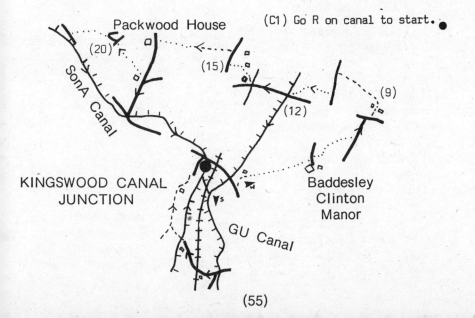

Packwood House
(20)
SonA Canal
(15)
(12)
(9)
KINGSWOOD CANAL JUNCTION
Baddesley Clinton Manor
GU Canal

THE WALK(S)

A main walk of 7.5 miles (Route (A) with cut off alternatives, Route (B) 4.5 miles and (C) 6 miles. All have a boggy bit. There are two canals, two historic houses and a grand avenue of trees. The first house is the moated Baddesley Clinton Manor which was started in the mid 1400's and occupied by the Roman Catholic Ferrers family until 1940, passing to the National Trust in 1980. It is a comly rural place with its oak panelling and chimney pieces, stained armorial glass, priest holes and walled garden.

The other mansion is Packwood House, also National Trust. Taller and more angular than Baddesley, with ranks of pointed gables, it was built in brick by John Featherstone in the early 1600's. However two large imitations, the Great Hall and the Long Gallery, were added in the 1930's, and these blunt my interest in the rest. But I would travel any summer weekend to see the walled garden where they play traditional jazz on a June night.

(1) From picnic area, get on towpath & go R to cross bridge. Take L fork 300 yds to GU Canal

(2) Go L appx 330 yds to bridge & onto road. Go R appx 200 yds, pass speed limit & take track L

(3) Follow to end & take stile to yard. Cross to R corner of building & take stile.

(4) Cross field diagonally (under power lines) to far R corner, & take stile. Follow R hedge to brook & take stiles. ◀

(5) Keep same line past manor to wood corner & on midfield to stile & drive.

(6) Go a few paces L, take public gate R & follow fenced path to lane.

(7) Go L, pass lane L & on 100 yds to bend. Enter farm gate L.

(8) Follow drive & take gates (1) & (2). Go ahead a few paces, but bear L to gate (3). Cross FENCE at plank L of gate. ▶

►(9) Follow hedged track appx .5 mile;
- at boggy patch keep R
- pass long pond R
- watch for pond L & take
        path on its bank,
& on to reach road.

(10) Go L appx 300 yds & take gate R. Go with hedge on your R to field corner. Cross bank ahead to next field.

(11) Go diagonally L (over middle fence) to field corner by bridge, & exit via railings to road.
    Route (A) - next para (12)

****
Route (B)
(11a) Join canal & go L (DOWNSTREAM) appx 1 mile to canal junction.

(11b) Go R to start.
****

(12) Go R appx .3 mile, cross railway & take track R.

(13) Follow to gate & take path on its R. Round house via gate & stiles, then on field edge to gate & track.

(14) Cross to R & take kissing gate. Go ahead up field edge to lane. ◢

(15) Go R appx 200 yds & take stile L to tree avenue. Follow appx .75 mile to lane & house.

(16) Go L appx .3 mile to road junction.
    Route (A) - next para (17)

****
Route (C)
(16a) Follow lane ahead .3 mile to road junction & join canal.

(16b) Go L (DOWNSTREAM) appx 1 mile to start.
****

(17) Take steps & stile R. Pass R of house to field. Follow field edge path over brook & stile.

(18) Go R along hedge, round field corner & on to take midhedge stile R.

(19) Go with hedge on your L. As it bends L, keep your line to far L corner gate & lane.

(20) Take lane opposite & just before house, take gate L. Go with hedge on your R, curving R to corner & thro hedge gap.

(21) Go with hedge on your L & take corner gate, then hedge on your R to gate/stile & B4439.

(22) Go L appx 75 yds & take track R to canal. Go L (DOWNSTREAM) 1.8 miles to start ●

WHERE
Map reference SP 171515, Landranger 151 Stratford upon Avon. A picnic site on a lane between Clifford Chambers, just south of Stratford upon Avon, and Welford on Avon. Buses run - details 0926 412929.

PARK & PICNIC
There is parking space on one side of the lane and some tables on the other.

MILCOTE STATION
The picnic site was once Milcote Station on the Great Western line from Stratford to Cheltenham, and the Cornishman express used to roar through from Birmingham. The line closed in 1976 and now there is nothing of it but the formation and the remains of a platform.

The platform is marked by a row of mature Corsican Pines which are an unusual and welcome feature in a pretty flat landscape. There is a rim of hills in every direction but Milcote is on a plain of wheat and barley and skylarks.

Stratford on Avon District Council turned the railway into a walking, cycling and riding route with an excellent all weather surface. In its 5 miles from Stratford to Long Marston you get quite pleasant views, since the embankment is above the surrounding land. The job included some planting with beech and hawthorne, hazel, elm and wild cherry. And you will see white campion and purple tree mallow. This looks amazingly like the

Lavatara which has become so popular in gardens,
and they are close relatives.

The Walks both pass along the south bank of the
River Avon, here up to 30 yards wide. It is an
angling, walking and boating river which is
navigable south to the Severn at Tewksbury. At
Stratford it is joined by the Stratford Canal and
so forms a useful link in the waterway system.
North of Stratford the Avon is not open to powered
boats, but you can hire rowing boats and punts.
From hard experience I recomend oars. Punting is a
sweaty and anxious business on a river with this
current. For all that, the Avon is placid and
smooth compared with the more powerful Severn.

You don't really need me to say anything about
Stratford upon Avon do you .....?

TWO WALKS WITH OPTIONS
There is no good Stroll-length circular outing from
Milcote, but many people wander down the old track
for a while, then wander back.

You could whiz up the line to Stratford and back,
about 6 miles without needing me. Here are two
other Walks; (A) 6 miles (with an optional extra
mile into Stratford and (B) 4 miles. If you link
them you get (A) + (B), a 7 mile walk because they
have some sections in common.

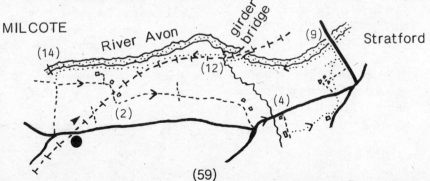

*
ALL START

(1) Take track on car park side of road appx .4 mile, crossing 1st track to 2nd by house.

Walk (A) next para (2)
Walk (B) next para (2a)
For (A) + (B) para (2)

(2) Go R & follow track appx 1.25 miles to road.

****
WALK (B) ONLY
(2a) Continue on railway appx 1 mile to cross FIRST BRIDGE over river (not big girder bridge). JUST after go L & take footbridge to field.
next para (12)◄
****

(3) Go L 400 yds, cross river bridge & take next track R.

(4) Go to Shire Horse Centre buildings & turn L towards car park. Take field path with hedge on your L, later on your R. Pass house & bear R with hedge to field corner.

(5) Go 40 paces along hedge to power pole, then bear L to far R field corner stile & road.

(6) Go to drive opposite & cross iron fence on R of gate. Cross field diagonally & take gate. ◄

(7) Go ahead to track then R past white house & brick house to enter field. Bear L (off track) & go with HEDGE on your L to take field corner gate.

(8) Go down with hedge on your R & join path to embankment. Go L to river.
OPTION
Go R into Stratford & return.

(9) Follow river bank path appx 1 mile downstream. Pass girder bridge, go on 150 yds to small bridge & join railway.

WALK (A) only next para (10)
FOR (A) + (B) next para (11)

(10) Go L appx 2 miles to start
****

(11) Go L (check - L) appx 200 yds to bridge. Just before it go R over footbridge to field.

►(12) Go L along bank to HEDGE (not fence) & take gate. Cross field to FAR R corner & take stile.

(13) Follow riverbank path .75 mile to weir & lock.

(14) Follow path away from river & L up field edge to meet track. Go L appx .6 mile & pass houses to old railway.

(15) Go R appx .4 mile to start

WHERE
Map reference SO 940750, Landranger 139 Birmingham.
A wood 3 miles north west of Bromsgrove just west
of Catshill. Buses run to within a mile. (Enquiries
0905 766802.)

PARK & PICNIC
There is a small car park, make sure that you take
one space not two. For a picnic, take the path left
from the car park, about 125 paces.

THE WOOD
Since 1981 Pepper Wood has been a "Community
Woodland" owned by the Woodland Trust and cared for
by a local group. I am grateful to the WT for
permission to use the wood as a picnic place.

Pepper Wood with nearby Chaddesley Woods, Big Wood,
Randan Wood and Waterpit Coppice are remnants of
the forest which once covered central England. From
Norman times they were part of the Forest of
Feckenham which covered north Worcestershire until
the 1600's.

Most of Pepper Wood is managed as "coppice with
standards". Trees are cut back every 15 years so
that they shoot from the base to grow sticks and
poles, with selected trees allowed to mature. This
system creates light shade, protective cover and a
rich habitat for plants, insects and animals. Part
of the wood is "high forest" where smaller trees
are felled to make room for the rest, and the
northern section is being left to itself.

There are 134 acres of oak with some ash and beech.
The understorey has hazel, hawthorne and birch.
Look out for bilberry and bluebells and wood
anemones, like a scatter of white stars in spring.
Higher up, tangling and twinning through the
bushes, embracing the trees and scenting the wood,
is honeysuckle. Watch for White Admiral and
Brimstone butterfies, greenfinches, goldfinches,
long tailed tits, and muntjac deer. To find out
about them get The Woodland Trust leaflet.

THE STROLL
You can wander round as you like, but here is a 1.5
mile circuit.

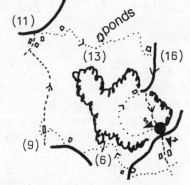

PEPPER WOOD

(1) At car park, put your back
to entrance & take path L.

(2) Follow through coppiced
area, cross small stream, pass
wooden barrier & path L, pass
house L, to end of track.

(3) Go R down track to start.●

THE WALK
About 4.5 miles with two farmyards, views south to
the Malverns, miles of delighful pastureland, a
long green lane and rolling Worcestershire hills.

(1) From car park, exit to road
& take farm drive opposite.

(2) Go thro farm plus 1 field &
take gate. Go R on field edge &
take stile.

(3) Cross midfield & take
stile, then on same line to
stile (L of gate) & lane.

(4) Go R, take 1st stile L.
Pass brick shed on your L &
take stile opposite shed door.➤

(5) Go with hedges on your R via 2 stiles, then with stream on R to bridge.

(6) Cross & take gate. Go up UNDER CABLES JUST L OF RIGHT ANGLE, & take gate to lane.

(7) Go R, pass house R & take stile in R hedge.

(8) Go L & cross field to take stile. Go up, making for far end of dutch barn, & take gate to drive.

(9) Take gate opposite, go round corner of farmhouse, & on to take field bottom gate.

(10) Go with hedge on your L, later on green lane, appx .75 mile, then round R bend & thro farm to lane.

(11) Go R to just past house R & take stile/gate R. Go upfield towards pylon, but take stile in hedge L.

(12) Cross field top & take far corner stile. Go with hedge on your L for 2 fields & take corner stile.

(13) Go L with hedge past ponds & take gate. Go ahead down midfield & take gate opposite.

(14) Go with hedge on your L, fully round R bend & take stile

(15) Keep same line to meet hedge L. Take track L past houses to lane.

(16) Go R to wood. Take middle of 3 entrances & follow track to car park.

Pipers Hill

WHÉRE
Map reference SO 958650, Landranger 150 Worcester &
the Malverns. Woodland on a hilltop 4 miles south
of Bromsgrove on the B4091.

PARK & PICNIC
There are parks at the north and south ends of the
wood, another in the middle is rather rough. The
notes below assume you are using the south park
(furthest from Bromsgrove). For an open wood there
are surprisingly few good siting places because
most of the ground is deep with leaf litter and
shaded. I recomend the little grassy knoll reached
via paragraphs (1) and (2) of the Stroll. There is
grass near the northern car park if you prefer it.

THE HILL, THE CHURCH, THE HALL & THE CUT
Piper's Hill is a steep sided sandstone mound about
350 feet high topped with a mature beech wood. Like
the nearby hill on which Hanbury Church stands (300
feet) it gives tremendous views across a landscape
that is grassland and ploughed, wooded and open,
hilly and flat, reaching faintly away to a distant
ring of hills. To the west are the humped Abberley
Hills and Titterstone Clee with the great hump of
Brown Clee. To the south west are the alpine
looking Malverns. Further south you can make out
Bredon Hill, a big undramatic dome, and to the
south east traces of the Cotswolds.

Hanbury Hall is a National Trust property. The Walk
takes you across the park and past the gate, so you
can see the brick and sandstone facade. It

was completed in about 1701 for Thomas Vernon but
the identity of the architect is unknown. There is
a warm and comfortable feeling about Hanbury Hall.
It is opulent and grand to be sure, but not big or
bad manered enough to dominate.

The Walk briefly follows the Worcester & Birmingham
Canal on its way to the River Severn. It was built
between 1791 and 1815 to take Birmingham metal
goods and coal, wood and farm produce. You meet
two locks on this short section but there are
another 56, mostly between Bromsgrove and Worcester
at the sharp fall from the Birmingham plateau.
Commercial traffic continued until 1964, mainly for
the Cadbury's works at Bournville and Worcester.

Hanbury Church stands on the site of an Iron Age
fort, which was followed by a Saxon monastry.
Parts of the present building date from about 1210
but its general character is 18th century. Inside
is light, reason and decent proportions. Get the
leaflet from the church for more details, and mind
that you give more than the 5 pence they ask.

THE STROLL
A 1.25 mile circuit from the south car park.

(1) At T junction of road &
lane, face road & go R appx 5ᴑ
paces. Cross & enter wood thro
wooden posts.

(2) Bear L & go parallel with
undergrowth to grassed hill top
area.

Picnic

(3) Face church & find path
down in that direction, to
track. ◢

(4) Go R to island & 2 footpath
signs.

(5) Take path R, pass pond &
track R & take path (L or R
fork) to green with 2 cottages.

(6) Go sharp R & take wood edge
FP to car park & road.

(7) Take path opposite along
wood edge & join track back to
start. ●

(65)

THE WALK
About 5 miles, visiting Hanbury Church, the Hall and the Canal.

✱

[Paras (1) to (4) as Stroll]

(5) From grass island take track L & path to church.

(6) Pass church on your L & follow lane down to junction.

(7) Take stile opposite, go ahead on field path to line of oaks, & take gate/stile.

(8) Go on to take next gate/stile. Bear L & walk with oaks on your R, pass (dry?) ponds & take kissing gate.

(9) Keep same line past front of house to opposite brick orangery (trees across front).

(10) Put your back to it & ahead sight pond with circle of trees. Then look R along line of hedge. Make for its R end where it meets bushes.

(11) Take stile to road then stile R. Cross paddock & take stile to field.

(12) Go R along field edges via stiles/gates appx .6 mile to gate R, & take STILE AHEAD.

(13) Cross field diagonally via stile & take corner bridge. Cross midfield to canal. ◀

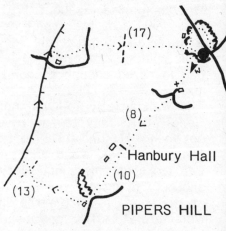

Hanbury Hall

PIPERS HILL

(14) Go R (UPSTREAM) appx .4 mile & under bridge, then on appx 100 yds to take stile R.

(15) Go with hedge on your R via bridge to gate/stile & cross midfield to stile & lane.

(16) Go R a few paces & take gate L. Go with hedge on your L, via gate & cross track.

(17) Go with hedge on your L towards field corner but take stile L, then 2nd stile.

(18) Go with hedge on your R via 3 fields & take iron stile to wood.

(19) Go ahead to main path then R, pass pond & track R & take path (L or R fork), to green with 2 cottages.

NEXT - Stroll paras (6) & (7). ▶

(66)

Pound Green

WHERE
Map reference SO 753788, Landranger 138 Kidder-
-minster & Wyre Forest. A clearing in the Wyre
Forest. The best picnic place is the Forestry
Commission's Hawkbatch Picnic Area, SO 761777 on
the B4194 west of Bewdley.

Buses run, details - 0299 404740. Alternativly,
catch a steam train from Bewdley or Bridgnorth,
when they are running (enquiries 0299 403816) and
get off at Arley to join the Walk at para (5a).

PARK & PICNIC
Hawkbatch site has car space and a few tables, or
you can picnic on the grass. Both the Walk and the
Stroll visit Pound Green.

POUND GREEN
The Wyre Forest covers about 6000 acres of dry acid
soil in a very hilly landscape shaped by the ice
when it melted some 10,000 years ago. The Forestry
Commission have owned it since 1925 and there are
many acres of oak and beech, but the northern
section, which surrounds Pound Green, is mainly
Scots Pine, Norway Spruce, Douglas Fir and Larch.

Commons are often owned by Parish Councils or local
trusts, but historically they belonged to the Lord
of the Manor. The "commoners" were local people who
had legal rights over them for limited purposes,
such as pasture. Pound Green Common is still
privately owned and there are eight commoners whose
rights derive from their properties on it.

The Common tops a crest on the west side of the
Severn Valley at about 300 feet. It may be a sea of
waving green bracken, or a wintry mixture of
yellows, red, dying orange and dusky brown.
Crowding round on two sides are the massed oaks and
sage green conifers of the Forest. Pound Green is
within a sack like enclave, open only in the north
towards Arley. The boundary between Worcestershire
and Shropshire runs down the west side. The Common
is one of the clearings in the Wyre which have not
changed much since the Domesday survey.

THE STROLL
About 2 miles. There are conifers, oak and birch, a
green lane and views of the forest treetops from
the Common.

(1) In parking area find
information board with map, &
take path behind.

(2) Pass 2 paths L & take 3rd.
Pass next path L to fork, go L
to grass ride with brick gizmo.

(3) Cross & go on to sharp R
bend, take path L. Curve R with
path & take next path L to
cross wood edge stile.

(4) Go with hedge on your L &
join green track. Follow via
gates to hard track, then to
track T junction. Go L to lane.

(5) Cross bearing R to take
gate/stile opposite. Make for
far R field corner & take stile

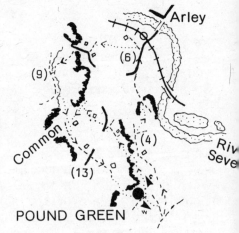

POUND GREEN

(6) Go ahead & pass house on
your R, to track by garden
fence corner.

(7) Go R past house, then bear
L on path to meet path. Go L
across common to stone shed.
[next Walk Para (12)]►

(68)

THE WALK:

Under 5 miles and mainly woodland, with oaks, beech and conifers in turn. From the Common and the northern part of the walk, there are views of the forest, Trimpley Reservoir and the Severn Valley, with the cast iron arch of Victoria Bridge carrying the railway over the Severn. Expect some mud. At one point a sign directs you to the Seckley Beech, a many branched, carved and initialed old veteran - when it was standing. You can see what's left.

(1) Go to end of car park & turning circle. Take path with red/green/white banded post.

(2) Follow to T junction, go R to pole barrier & main track.

(3) Go L, take gate & follow track .7 mile (pass brick gizmos) to 5 track junction.

(4) Go ahead appx 32 paces & take small path R. Follow (past Seckley Beech dec'd on L) appx .4 mile to track & gate.

(5) Go ahead via gate to lane. Go R to R bend with 2 beeches & track L.

Arley ◀

{ (5a) IF STARTING FROM STATION, }
{ exit to lane & go R over rail }
{ bridge to 1st track R. }

(6) Take stile opposite trees. Go with hedge on your R, round 2 corners & take corner stile (?bust). Stay with hedge R .3 mile & take gate R to track.

(7) Go L to lane, then R to wood corner & take track L.

(8) Follow via R bend & gate, past track L, to R bend over stream & T junction.

(9) Go L appx 250 yds & take path L by wooden post.

(10) Cross stile & stream, then with stream on your R. Cross plank bridge & go 12 paces on, to wooden post L. ▶

(11) Go R, path joins wooden fence R, pass green shed R, & keep same path to stone shed L.

(12) Take path ahead to track. Go L past houses to T junction with lane.

(13) Go R, take Woodhouse Farm gate L. Follow track past farm & take stile by gate ahead.

(14) Go with hedge on your L & take corner stile to wood. Follow path ahead, bearing L to T junction. Go R to start.

Seven Springs

WHERE
Map reference SK 205003, on the edges of Landranger 128 Derby & Burton on Trent and 127 Stafford & Telford. A picnic site off the A513 on the north east tip of Cannock Chase.

PARK & PICNIC
Parking space and tables provided by Staffs County Council, with another 26 square miles of Chase.

THE PLACE
There are notes on the Chase under Castle Ring, which is in the pines on the southern tip. Much of the north part of the Chase is exciting little sandy hills covered in heather and bilberry.

Seven Springs is a lovely spot but the points of interest are on the Walk. There are the stepping stones over the clear water of the Sher Brook, which you can follow to its source at a spring about 2.5 miles south.

You pass the gates of Shugborough Hall and later get a distant view from the canal. Built in 1693 it was extended and remodelled in the 1760's and is now houses Lord Lichfield and the County Museum. I find it lumpy and dissapointing, but it is worth a go-round to see the Museum and the extravagant stone follies in the grounds. Sleek trains on the main railway line between London and the North flash through a cutting and tunnel.

The Walk follows the last mile of the Staffs & Worcs Canal beside Tixall Wide, a beautiful lake section of the canal probably built to please the owner of Tixall Hall. After meeting the Trent & Mersey Canal, you pass the Essex Packhorse Bridge over the Trent.

THE STROLL
A 3 mile wander which explains the Seven Springs and takes you up to the tops for some views.

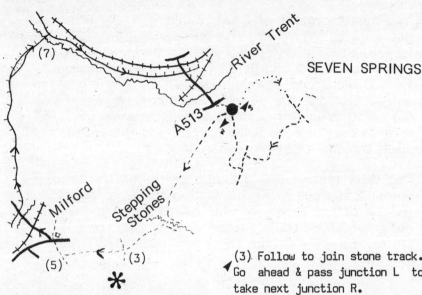

SEVEN SPRINGS

(3). Follow to join stone track.
Go ahead & pass junction L to
take next junction R.

(4) Follow up to crest & T
junction. Go L to junction.

(5) Take track R appx .5 mile
DOWN to start.

(1) Leave car park past pool on
L of entrance, & follow paths
thro wood & past streams to
meet boundary fence.

(2) Go R, parallel with fence,
path becomes clearer & joins
path from R.

THE WALK
A walk of about 6.75 miles visiting the Stepping
Stones, some alarmingly steep hills, the Staffs &
Worcs and Trent & Mersey Canals, the River Trent
and a railway.

(1) In car park, put your back
to entrance & take track on R.
At pole barrier go R appx .5
mile to Stepping Stones.

(2) Cross & take track R, .4
mile to cross paths. (Punchbowl
R, Mere Pool L)

(3) Take steep path ahead up to
crest. Pass 2 paths from R &
old pines L.

(4) Cross a path & pass one
from R, then keep same line
down gulley, & on appx .3 mile
to T junction by pools L.

(72)

(5) Go R over crest & down to A513 opposite Shugborough gates

(6) Take lane L of gates to canal. Go R on towpath appx 2 miles to canal junction.

(7) Go R, pass lock & iron bridge & go appx 1 mile to next bridge by double power poles.

(8) Leave canal & go R to A513. Take track opposite to start.

Yarningdale Common

WHERE
Map reference SP 188658, Landranger 151 Stratford upon Avon. A hill about 3 miles east of Henley in Arden just north from the B4095. No buses.

PARK & PICNIC
Park near the road, then make for the crest of the hill and cast about for a place. There are a couple of benches.

THE COMMON
A well wooded hill some 360 feet high called Mill Mound sits snugly amongst other green and comely hills in this idyllic part of the Arden country.

Common land was not public, but belonged to the Lord of the Manor. The holders of adjacent land shared defined rights over it, such as a right to pasture cattle, take firewood or cut turves. Yarningdale Common is refered to in a document of 1482. The use of the common from year to year was decided at the Manor Court, but it has been a recreation area since at least the mid 1800's. The Lord of the Manor gave it to Claverdon Parish Council in 1950, and they manage it on the advice of Warwickshire Nature Conservation Trust.

Half a mile west the Stratford on Avon Canal
wanders dreamily round the hills, conceding an
occasional sleepy lock to change levels. From
Kings Norton, Birmingham it winds 22 miles with 15
locks through the southern suburbs of Birmingham
and into rural Warwickshire. Passing Earlswood and
Hockley Heath, the quaint junction with the Grand
Union Canal, Wootten Wawen and Wilmcote (home of
Shakspeare's mother - well it was once), it runs to
the centre of Stratford town and the River Avon.

The northern part had some commercial use into the
1950's but the Lapworth to Stratford section was
unused since the 1930's. Closure was proposed in
1955 but there was massive public protest and it
was taken over in 1960 by the National Trust.

Picnic here in high summer when the grass is long
and the air heavy. There are slow fat cows and
shimmering insects, air warm as breath, and hazy,
leafy tree tops.

THE STROLL
Under 2 miles, with cows and sheep, rough meadows,
the canal, three locks and an aqueduct.

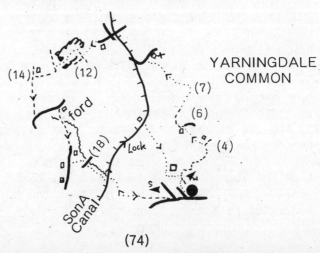

*

(1) Post box faces road at junction of road & lane. Follow ROAD down side of open area, pass 2nd lane R & take track R.

(2) Follow to end & take stile by L of 2 gates.

(3) Go with hedge on your R down 2 fields, to bottom of slope, & take gate/stile.

(4) Go R via hedge gap. Cross field to opposite corner & take gate to canal.

(5) Go R past 3 locks & on to red barn L by narrow neck of canal.

(6) Take stile R. Bear R, cross wood diagonally & take footbridge. ◢

(7) Cross midfield & take gate. Cross diagonally to meet hedge R & take top corner stile.

(8) Go with hedge on your R & take stile, then cross midfield to stile & track.

(9) Go L to farm & take lane R 100 yds. Take path R into wood.

(10) Follow main path, ignore small paths L & R, to junction with barrier R.

(11) Take path ahead, passing barrier on your R, to open area. Pass R fork & on thro barriers (1) & (2).

(12) Take either path down to road junction & post box. ●

*

THE WALK
Under 5 miles with pebbly, sandy tracks in long tunnels of trees, sheep pasture, the canal, part of the Heart of England Way, a ford and a reedy willowy stream. It can be muddy.

*

(1) From post box take path up hedge behind it, over plank bridge & up thro bushes.

(2) Pass thro 2 wooden barriers to open area. Bear R, pass 3rd wood barrier L & path R, & curve R to lane. ◢

(3) Go L down to farm, then R on track appx .5 mile to drive & house.

(4) Cross stile L & on to take next. Take stile R, follow line of R hedge to corner & keep same line via midfence stile (?bust), to field end gate (?bust). ▶

(75)

(5) Go up to R side of house. Cross "stile" to yard & lane.

(6) Go L on track (past track L) .5 mile, via double gates at bog, to end at field corner.

(7) Go L on field edge & take corner stile. Keep same line to cross field corner & join L hedge, then follow it & take corner stile.

(8) Go with hedge on your L, round field corner, & take stile L. Go ahead to end of fence R, then down to L side of church & take stile.

(9) Go L to canal & take small gate L to towpath. Go R via bridge & under next bridge, then exit R to lane.

(10) Cross canal to T junction. Take lane opposite 200 yds & take stile R.

(11) Go upfield with power lines via 2 stiles to track.

(12) Go R, cross barrier & take stile L. Follow wood edge & take stile into wood.

(13) Follow path thro to field L. Go R to track, then L via gates. Round R bend to gate & farm road.

(14) Go L appx .3 mile to lane. Go L .2 mile to house & track R

(15) Follow track via ford, appx .5 mile to start of lane.

(16) Go appx 150 yds to cottage R. Cross fence opposite & follow path to stile & field.

(17) Go down, pass gate L, to bottom corner stile & lane.

(18) Take stile opposite, follow line of stream on your L & take stile near footbridge.

(19) DON'T cross bridge, follow stream & take field end gate.

(20) Go thro thicket to canal & cross bridge to gate & field.

(21) Bear R to opposite corner. Go thro gap & take 1st gate L.

(22) Go up with hedge on your L 2 fields, & take stile to track

(23) Go ahead to common & postbox.

(76)